NATIONAL GEOGRAPHIC

School Publishing

Color and Size

Mary Garcia

PICTURE CREDITS

Illustrations by Mini Goss (4–5, 14–15).

Cover, Ibis for Kids Australia; 1, 6 (below left & above center), 7 (above left & below left), 8 (all), 10 (all), 12 (above right), 13 (above, left & right), 16 (above left, center left & center right), Lindsay Edwards Photography; 2, 9 (right), David Sanger Photography/Alamy; 6 (above right), 7 (right), 12 (left), 16 (above right), Getty Images; 9 (left), Detail Parenting/Alamy; 11 (left), 13 (center), 16 (below left), oote boe/Alamy; 11 (right), 16 (below right), Thinkstock/Alamy.

Produced through the worldwide resources of the National Geographic Society, John M. Fahey, Jr., President and Chief Executive Officer; Gilbert M. Grosvenor, Chairman of the Board; Nina D. Hoffman, Executive Vice President and President, Books and Education Publishing Group.

PREPARED BY NATIONAL GEOGRAPHIC SCHOOL PUBLISHING

Ericka Markman, Senior Vice President and President Children's Books and Education Publishing Group; Steve Mico, Senior Vice President and Publisher; Marianne Hiland, Editorial Director; Lynnette Brent, Executive Editor; Michael Murphy and Barbara Wood, Senior Editors; Bea Jackson, Design Director; David Dumo, Art Director; Margaret Sidlowsky, Illustrations Director; Matt Wascavage, Manager of Publishing Services; Sean Philpotts, Production Manager.

MANUFACTURING AND QUALITY MANAGEMENT

Christopher A. Liedel, Chief Financial Officer; Phillip L. Schlosser, Director; Clifton M. Brown III, Manager.

BOOK DEVELOPMENT

Ibis for Kids Australia Pty Limited.

Published by the National Geographic Society
1145 17th Street, N.W.
Washington, D.C. 20036-4688

ISBN 0-7922-6052-X

Third Printing 2008
Printed in China

Contents

tall ladder

yellow bananas

Open

Sale Today

short ladder

big dog

long legs

4

Clothing Store

green tree

Shoe Store

small dog

short legs

tall woman

short boy

5

Red

balls

toy cars

6

Is the red bear BIG or small?

teddy bears

7

Blue

Find the blue things.

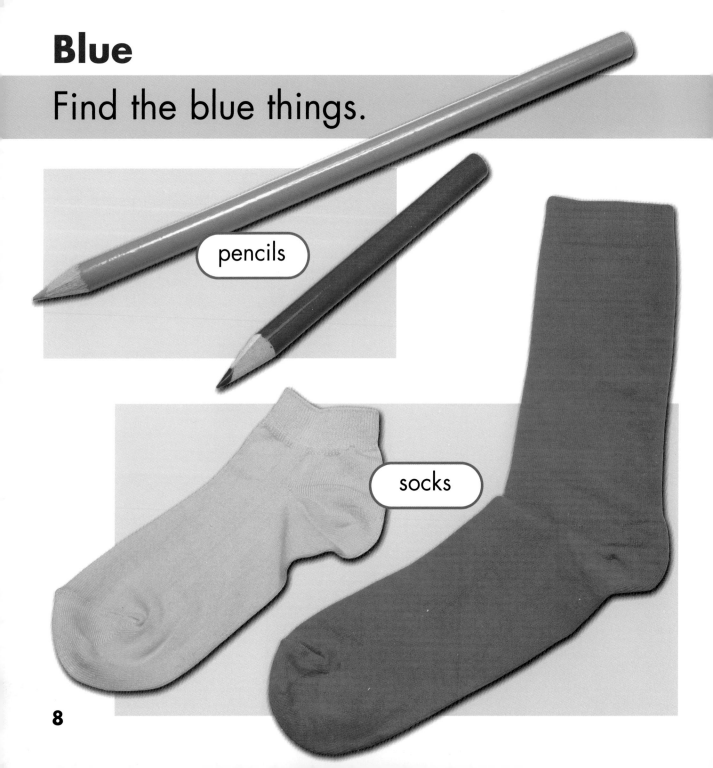

pencils

socks

Is the blue slide long or short?

slides

Find the yellow things.

candles

vases

Is the yellow ladder tall or short?

ladders

Different Colors, Different Sizes

Things are different colors.
Things are different sizes.

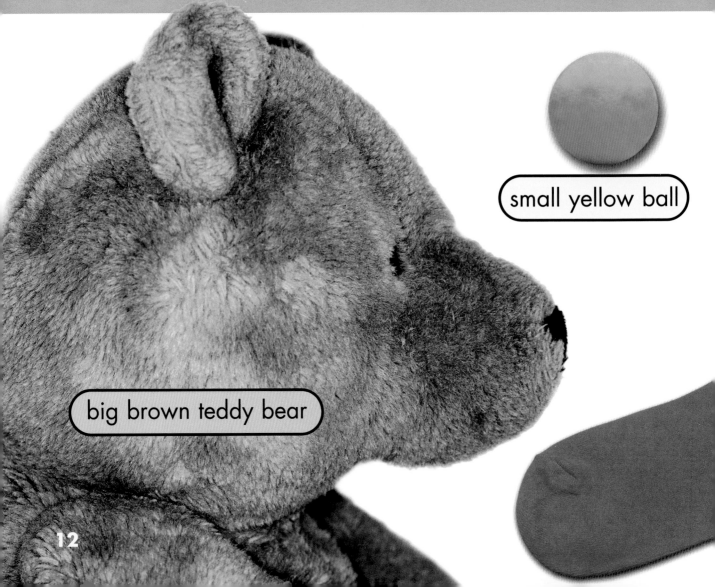

small yellow ball

big brown teddy bear

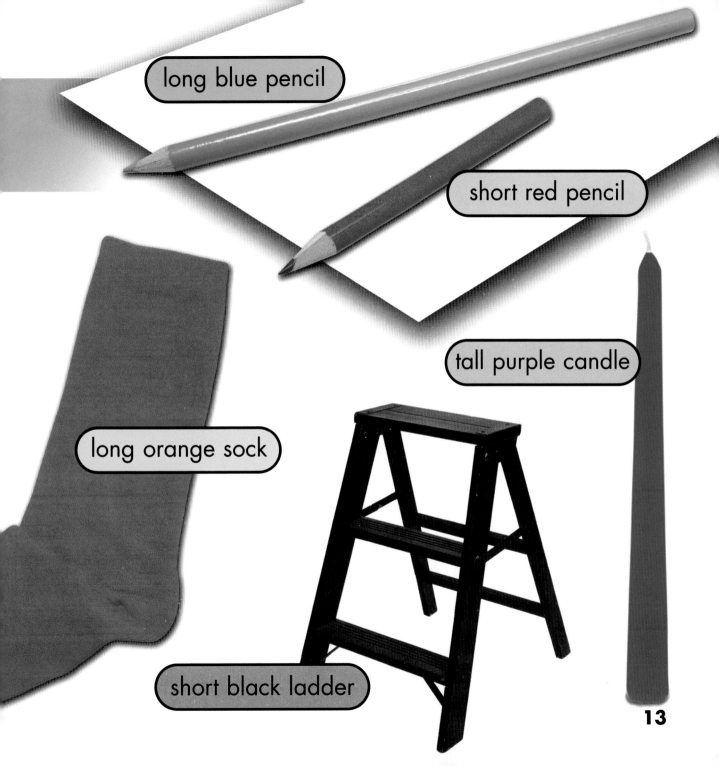

long blue pencil

short red pencil

tall purple candle

long orange sock

short black ladder

13

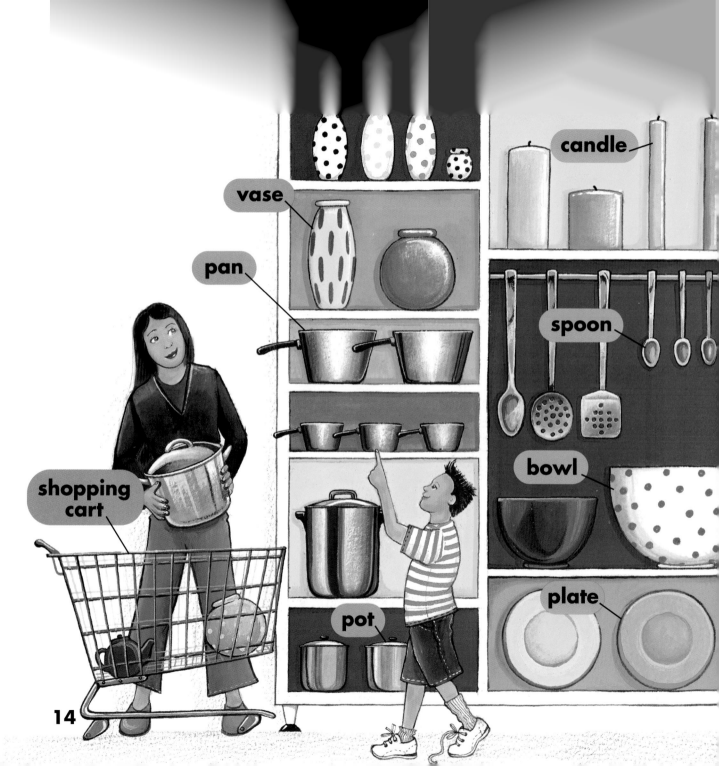

candle

vase

pan

spoon

bowl

shopping cart

plate

pot

14

Things are many different colors and sizes.
What different colors and sizes do you see?

teapot

pitcher

fork

glass

shelf

saucer

teacup

shopping basket

COLOR
black
blue
green
orange
purple
red
yellow

SIZE
big
long
short
small
tall

Picture Glossary

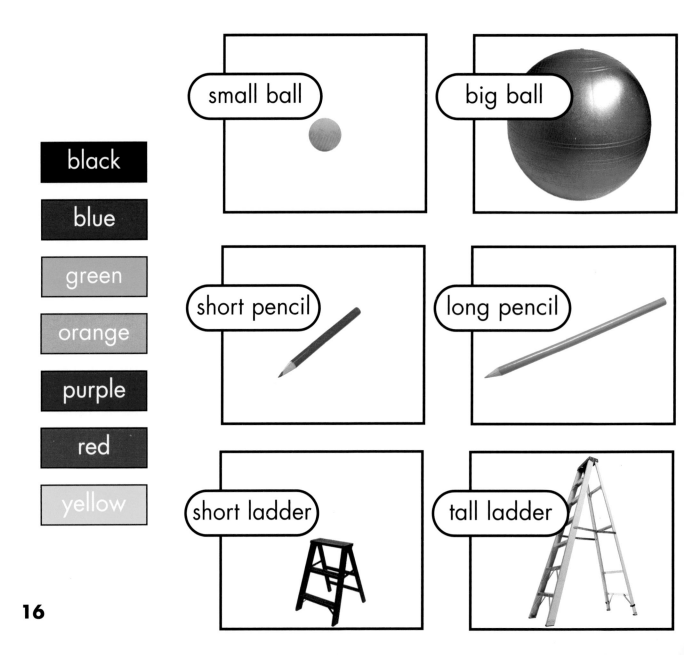

black

blue

green

orange

purple

red

yellow

small ball

big ball

short pencil

long pencil

short ladder

tall ladder